The Hero and the Healer

The Hero and the Healer

Aurora Raine

Revised version of Love Notes in Lullabies, 2019. No longer printed.

Copyright Aurora Raine, 2022.
All rights reserved.

ISBN: 9798437769966
Imprint: Independently published

Printed in the United States of America

Cover Image: Birmingham Museums Trust

No part of this publication may be reproduced, stored in or introduced into a retrieval system or transmitted, in any form, by any means. If taking photos of this book and any of it's pages to share on social media, please tag the author, Aurora Raine.

TABLE OF CONTENTS

Part One: The Spark

Come and Go..1
Explosions..2
Worth the Wait...3
A Chance...4
The Inbetween...5
Circles..6
Searching the Stars...7
Feelings..8
Same Moon..9
Next to Me...10
My Words...11
The Sun..13
Promise..14
Long Distance..15
Collide..16
In the Sun..17

Part Two: The Fire

It's You...24
Loved...26
Worth the Wait...27
A Storm is Coming...28
Forbidden Love..29
Hope..30
Catalyst..31

TABLE OF CONTENTS CONTINUED

Entwined..32
Comfort..33
The Hero and the Healer.............................34
A Quiet Love...35
Kiss...36
The Pull..37
As Love Should Be......................................38
Lifetimes..39
Written in the Stars....................................41
The Morning We Said Goodbye..................42

Part Three: The Ashes

In Your Name...48
Fighting Fate..49
Fighting Time...50
Stubborn Heart..51
With or Without You..................................52
My Answer...53
Running Away...54
Hands..55
Running On Empty....................................56
Aftermath..57
Silence...58
A Moment...59
Learning..60
My Greatest Act..61

TABLE OF CONTENTS CONTINUED

Under the Moon..62
Distance...63
Our Chapter..64
In the Next Lifetime..65
Sail...66
Remembrance...67
Slipping...69
Back to My Own Heart.....................................70
Wish..71
Pen...72
Alone in a Crowded Room...............................73
Foreigners..74
Face in the Crowd...75
The End of the Beginning.................................76
Find Me in the Future......................................77
Never Forget...78
Let You Go..79

PART ONE

*"Then birds flew up like a shower of
sparks, I followed them with my eyes
and saw how they rose in a single breath,
until they seemed no longer to be rising
but I to be falling..."*

– Franz Kafka

Aurora Raine

COME AND GO

He arrives
    when the summer heat wanes
    and red and orange hues
    paint the trees
And as the leaves fall, so do I
    descending, spiraling
    until I hit the ground
    hard enough to take my breath away
He leaves as quickly as he arrived
    and I am left
    in the bitter cold and brutal heat
    until he returns next time

EXPLOSIONS

The fire was roaring underneath the night sky
    Every star a reason why I never said
    The things I should have
I don't know why I stayed there, but I did
    Every connection between us
    Explosions you will never hear
My hands begging to touch your skin
    And kiss the poison from your lips

It took every ounce of me to walk away

Aurora Raine

WORTH THE WAIT

Darling,
    you will always be
    worth the wait
No matter what I do,
    I do not think my heart
    will ever not choose you

A CHANCE

If I had the chance
    I would love you so much
    you would have no choice
    but to love yourself
If only you could see you
    the way I do

THE INBETWEEN

we have always existed
    somewhere in between
not at the beginning
    never the end
just somewhere
    in between

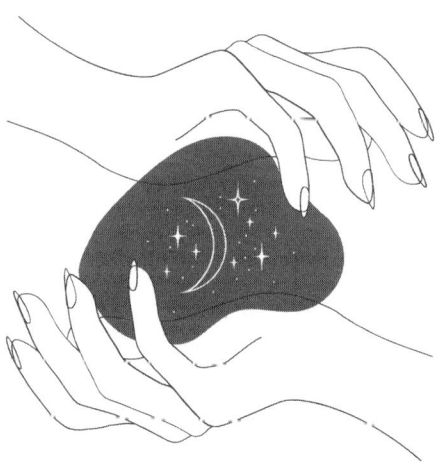

CIRCLES

my life
    it circles around and around
    back to you
and now I wait to see
    if you will come back around
    or if our time has run out

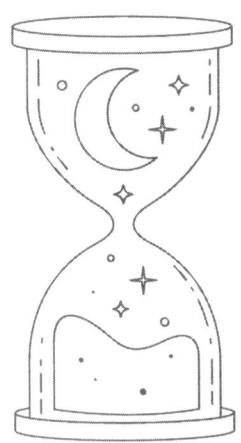

SEARCHING THE STARS

oh my love
where have you been
I have been searching for you
in the stars again

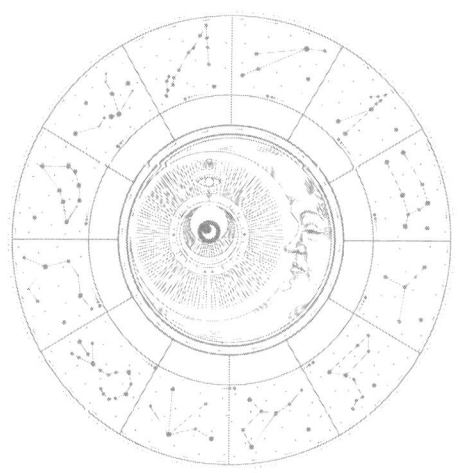

FEELINGS

I didn't ask
    for these feelings
therefore,
    I do not believe
    I can simply
    just ask for them to leave

SAME MOON

We may be
    in different cities
but as long as
    we are under the same moon
    then I know
    we still have a chance

NEXT TO ME

It doesn't matter
    where on Earth
    I plant my feet
as long as you are
    standing next to me

MY WORDS

I breathe you in
    and I breathe out
  poetry

THE SUN

When you are ready
   for the kind of love
   that feels like sunshine
  come and find me

PROMISE

I promise
> to always be a light
> when the darkness
> comes

LONG DISTANCE

I will always be
    your biggest fan
    cheering you on
    from a distance

COLLIDE

I am the sun
   and he is the moon
      and I am still trying
         to make our two worlds
      collide

IN THE SUN

I have only ever
   been able to love you
   under the moon
Imagine what it would have looked like
   in the sun

PART TWO

The Fire

"Last night I dreamed about you. What happened in detail I can hardly remember, all I know is that we kept merging into one another. I was you, you were me. Finally you somehow caught fire."

– Franz Kafka

IT'S YOU

It's who you think about when the rest of the world goes quiet around around you. It's who you think about in the dark before falling asleep. It's who affects you the most the next morning after dreaming about them. It's who makes you feel the most alive. It's who you think about when you look at the moon.
It's you. It's you. It's you.

Aurora Raine

LOVED

You will never
    not be loved by me.

                                       Not now.
                                       Not ever.

WORTH THE WAIT

Darling,
You will always be
   worth the wait
No matter what I do
   I do not think my heart
   will ever not choose you

A STORM IS COMING

You are a storm.
And I have never been
    afraid of thunder.

FORBIDDEN LOVE

It is
   in your arms
   I find my solace
your beating heart
   in unison with mine
our bodies tangled up
   in our own universe
where in this moment
   it does not feel
   like the whole world is against us

HOPE

Believe me,
    the last thing I know
    is how to make this work
but
believe me,
    being with you
    is what I know first.

The Hero and the Healer

CATALYST

At a time
    when I felt so caged
you brought out
    the wild in me
you gave me courage
    to be fearless
and made me feel alive
    and for that
I will be
    eternally thankful

ENTWINED

How do you do it
    make my whole body feel alive
like every cell
    is bursting and multiplying
like I could shoot stars
    straight from my eyes
I think maybe
    yours and my universes
    are intrinsically entwined

COMFORT

The comfort we feel with one another is no accident.
I believe we are meant to help one another grow into
the people we are meant to become.
The people we always were underneath.

Aurora Raine

THE HERO AND THE HEALER

Rest your shaking
   hands in mine
Let me envelop
   your weary soul
   with the warmth of my body
and heal the places
   that have been broken
   for far too long

A QUIET LOVE

We loved quietly
but it felt
oh so very
loud

KISS

If my words ever fail
    to explain how I feel
Let my kiss
    tell you all
        you need to know

THE PULL

You
will always
keep being pulled
to the person with whom you belong

Aurora Raine

AS LOVE SHOULD BE

I do not need you to save me. I saved myself a long time ago. And I do not want to save you. I accept you as you are as love should be. I just want someone by my side to go on wild adventures with, and to feel at home with, all the while feeling free and at peace.

LIFETIMES

It has always been you.

Centuries ago
    and lifetimes to come.

It will still be you.

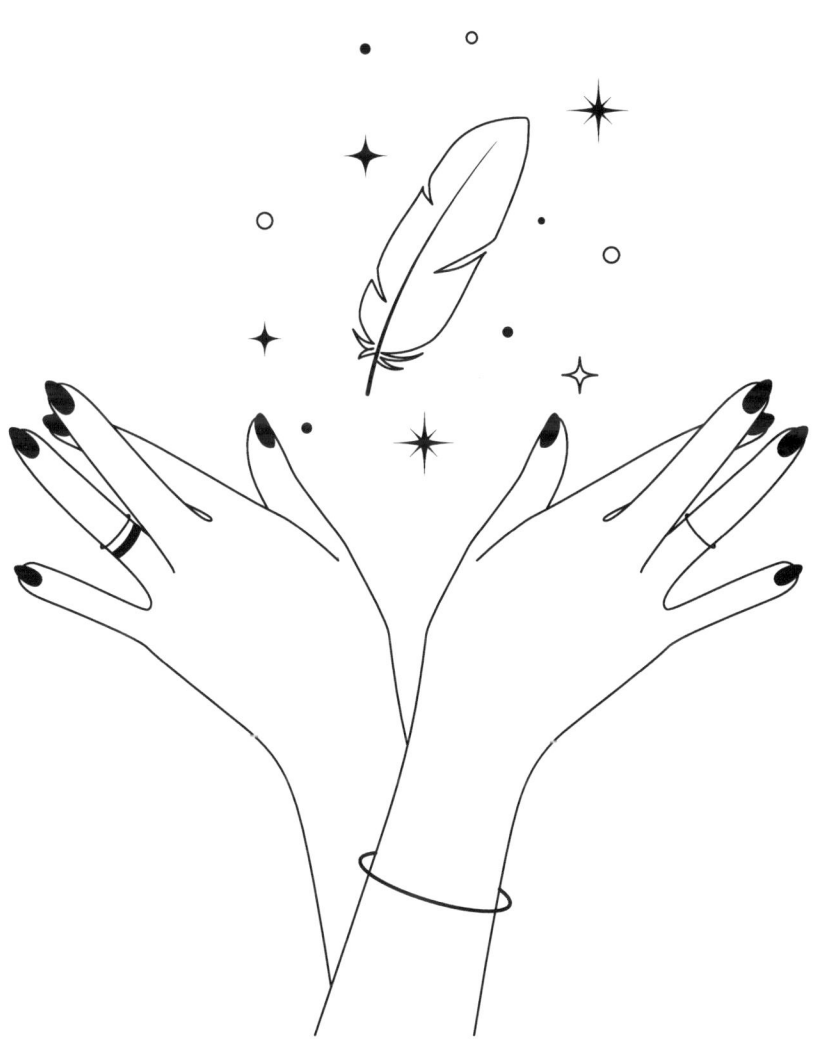

WRITTEN IN THE STARS

I couldn't quiet this love
    even if I tried
    oh and believe me I did
Our names were written in the stars
Your soul's frequency
    in tune with mine
I have waited for a love like this
    my whole life
    so pure
    so divine
I will be there in our next lifetime
    and maybe then
    we will align

Aurora Raine

THE MORNING WE SAID GOODBYE

Closed eyes, your hand in mine
    in the night we stayed alive
stitching our bodies together
    only for them to be ripped apart
the next morning

PART THREE

The Ashes

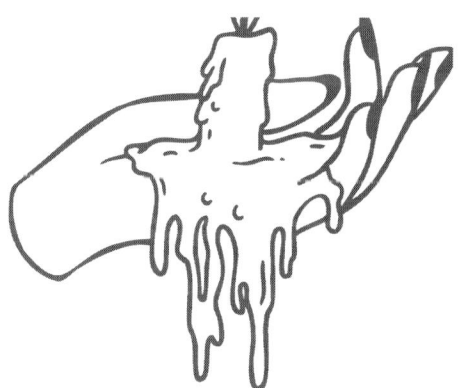

"But what if all the tranquility, all the comfort, all the contentment were now to come to a horrifying end?"

– Franz Kafka

IN YOUR NAME

we should have known
a spark like this
was enough to cause
an explosion

and even now
as we wait for the dust to settle
I would still
set the world on fire
in your name

FIGHTING FATE

I will
    fight fate
I will go against
    space and time
Dive into a black hole
Just to find my way
    back to you

Aurora Raine

FIGHTING TIME

Time is not on our side
It never has been
    and I know this storm
    seems to never end
But it's coming
    our time is coming

STUBBORN HEART

The universe
    must be really tired
        of fighting
            my stubborn heart

WITH OR WITHOUT YOU

If you want me to be honest
    know that I am completely terrified
    of being with you
    of being without you

MY ANSWER

In your silence,
    I found my answer.

RUNNING AWAY

There is
    so much more to say
    so much more to do
but here we go
    running away
    before we are through

HANDS

You only wanted me
    when your hands were empty
But all you did
    was make my hands empty too

RUNNING ON EMPTY

How exhausting it is
    to keep running from
    and running to you
    at the same time

AFTERMATH

I am drowning
   in the aftermath

            of the hurricane
                  that was us

Aurora Raine

SILENCE

I loved you in silence
    for so much of my life

           and back to the silence
               is where I now go

A MOMENT

I will never regret
   loving you
   just to lose you
Every moment was worth it
   even if it was only for
   a moment.

LEARNING

You asked me how I was; I said fine,
    but what I really meant was
I am learning how to live
    without you.

MY GREATEST ACT

I am going to tell you this isn't hurting me.
I am going to pretend I am fine.
I am going to act as though
    every cell in my body
    isn't in love with the mere existence of you.
and it is going to be my greatest act.

UNDER THE MOON

I forget you in the morning sun
   only to remember you
  under the moon.

DISTANCE

There is an unfathomable distance between us
but the bridge is still standing
and the streetlight is still on

OUR CHAPTER

I like to think that one day
    You will come back to me
    Like forgetting a book you were reading
    And turning back to our chapter
    We never got to completing

IN THE NEXT LIFETIME

If our souls
    can keep finding one another
    again and again
    in this lifetime
surely they can do so
    in the next

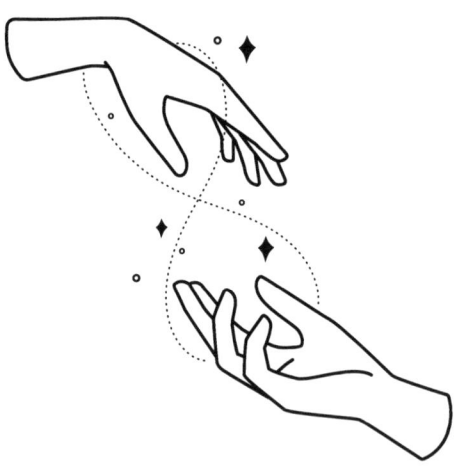

SAIL

I am envious
    of the moon
        that pulls the tide with ease
If I could do the same
    I would sail you back to me.

REMEMBRANCE

autumn leaves fall
the colors change; for me
    and you
one year has passed
now the sun envelopes the moon; a hello
    and goodbye
    said in the same sentence
two worlds colliding into remembrance
    for only a moment
as everything grows cold around us
    we are reminded
    this was never meant to last

SLIPPING

I can feel you slipping through my fingers
    like sand in the palm of my hand
    my compass is no longer pointed at you
    and the lighthouse light has long burned out
You are not the brightest star in my sky
    nor the wind in my sails
I cast you now from me
    like an arrow pulled straight from my chest
I have been hurting long enough

BACK TO MY OWN HEART

You left me in darkness
   but I followed the stars
      I followed a constellation
         that led me back to my own heart

WISH

I let you go
like blowing the seeds
from a dandelion–

with one last wish.

PEN

All you are to me now
    are words on paper
and I will always
    have a part of you
as long as
    I am holding
    this pen

ALONE IN A CROWDED ROOM

You would have had anyone
    your shaking hands reached for softer skin
    loneliness etched at your side
    I could see it when you walked
In the crowded room, your eyes
    searched for anyone
    for no one
    for mine
We shut them all out with the music
    dancing alone in a crowded room
    until it was only me and you
Our hands
    reached
    reached
    touched.

Do you remember when I told you I wouldn't let you
fall into the fire when you wanted to jump?
Why did you let me jump with you?

Do you still hear the music?

FOREIGNERS

Your hands are too foreign
   your mouth too familiar
   your eyes meant to gaze into another's
I'm so sorry for thinking of you
   when I shouldn't be thinking of you
Dreaming of you
   when I shouldn't be dreaming of you
You know I shouldn't be thinking of you
I'm so sorry for thinking of you

Where are you
Where are you
Where are you
Where are you
Where are you

FACE IN THE CROWD

I think of you on cold mornings
    when my coffee cup no longer warms my hands
    when the rain pitter patters
    on the tin roof outside of my window
    and I am out of my last drink
You are a sentence in a book I read
    lyrics in a song I can't bring myself to sing
    you are a face in the crowd
    on the sidewalk down the street
When I look into a strangers eyes
    it is yours I wish I could see

THE END OF THE BEGINNING

I am keeping the book open
This is not how our story will end

FIND ME IN THE FUTURE

In the future
You will find me waiting
In a little cottage by the sea
My field of sunflowers
Will have reached their way up
To touch the turquoise sky
I will have left the kettle on for you
And a little candle in the window
And we will laugh about
How we thought for a moment
Everything was lost
When all you needed to do was
Find me
In the Future

NEVER FORGET

I will never forget the love we almost had.

LET YOU GO

I no longer know how to love you
and so,
I must let you go.

"Every thing you love is very likely to be lost, but in the end, love will return in a different way."

– Franz Kafka

ABOUT THE AUTHOR

Aurora Raine is a poetry and fiction writer, from a small town in West Virginia, who currently resides in Pittsburgh, Pennsylvania.

She is the mother of four children.

She owns the independent bookstore, Wildflowers and Ink. She enjoys reading, traveling, and spending time with family.

You can find her on Instagram as @auroraraine_poetry. For more information, events, and more, visit: www.auroraraine.com.

Printed in Great Britain
by Amazon